VESTAVIA HILLS
RICHARD M. SCRUSHY
PUBLIC LIBRARY

1112 Montgomery Highway
Vestavia Hills, Alabama 35216

Reptiles and Amphibians

ANIMAL FACTS

by Heather C. Hudak

WEIGL PUBLISHERS INC.

Published by Weigl Publishers Inc.
350 5th Avenue, Suite 3304, PMB 6G
New York, NY 10118-0069 USA
Web site: www.weigl.com

Copyright 2005 WEIGL PUBLISHERS INC.
All rights reserved. No part of this publication may be reproduced, stored
in a retrieval system, or transmitted in any form or by any means, electronic,
mechanical, photocopying, recording, or otherwise, without the prior written
permission of the publisher.

Library of Congress Cataloging-in-Publication Data

Hudak, Heather C., 1975-
  Reptiles and amphibians / Heather C. Hudak.
     p. cm. -- (Animal facts)
  Includes index.
  ISBN 1-59036-204-7 (library binding : alk. paper) 1-59036-246-2 (softcover)
  1. Reptiles--Juvenile literature. 2. Amphibians--Juvenile literature. I. Title.
  QL644.2.H74 2004
  597.9--dc22
                              2004001996

Printed in the United States of America
1 2 3 4 5 6 7 8 9 0   08 07 06 05 04

Project Coordinator Heather C. Hudak   **Substantive Editor** Heather Kissock
Copy Editor Donald Wells   **Design** Janine Vangool   **Layout** Bryan Pezzi
Photo Researcher Ellen Bryan

Photograph and Text Credits
Every reasonable effort has been made to trace ownership and to obtain
permission to reprint copyright material. The publishers would be pleased
to have any errors or omissions brought to their attention so that they may
be corrected in subsequent printings.

Cover: A.B. Sheldon; **Corel Corporation:** pages 6T, 6M, 7T, 7MT, 7MB, 15T, 16, 17L;
DigitalVision: page 18; **David Liebman:** page 6B; **Dan Nedrelo:** pages 17B, 19B;
Photos.com: pages 5, 11R, 20, 22; **Photodisc:** page 9L; **Photospin:** pages 1, 15B, 23;
A. B. Sheldon: pages 4, 8, 9R, 12, 13, 14T, 14B; **Tom Stack & Associates:** page 17T
(Kitchin & Hurst); **J. D. Taylor:** pages 3, 7B, 10, 11L, 19T.

All of the Internet URLs given in the book were valid at the time of publication.
However, due to the dynamic nature of the Internet, some addresses may have
changed, or sites may have ceased to exist since publication. While the author
and publisher regret any inconvenience this may cause readers, no responsibility
for any such changes can be accepted by either the author or the publisher.

Contents

What Are Reptiles
and Amphibians? 4

Reptile and Amphibian Families 6

Reptile and
Amphibian Appearances 8

Ancient Amphibian
and Reptile Relics 10

Life Cycle 12

Lizard Lairs and
Salamander Shelters 14

Snake Snacks and Frog Fare 16

Threatened Reptiles
and Amphibians 18

Activities 20

Quiz 22

Further Reading/Web Sites 23

Glossary/Index 24

What Are Reptiles and Amphibians?

Glass frogs are named for their clear skin. They are also known as ghost frogs.

A reptile is an animal that has dry, scaly skin. An amphibian is an animal that has moist, smooth skin. Reptiles and amphibians are cold-blooded animals. This means that their body temperature is the same as their environment. These animals must lie in the Sun to warm up. They lie in the shade to cool off.

Reptiles and amphibians live in every part of the world except Antarctica. Reptiles live in mountains, forests, oceans, and deserts. Amphibians live near lakes, rivers, and ponds. They live the first part of their lives in the water. They spend the second part on land.

Reptiles and amphibians have lived on Earth for millions of years. Today, there are about 6,000 reptile species and about 4,000 amphibian species. Each of these animals has special features. These features help them to survive in different climates and **habitats**.

Chameleons can change color to blend in with their environment.

Fast Facts

The word amphibian comes from the Greek words *amphi* and *bios*. Amphi means "both." Bios means "life."

About 15 percent of snakes have venom that is harmful to humans.

Herpetology is the study of reptiles and amphibians.

Reptiles and amphibians are vertebrates. This means they have a backbone. Amphibians are the smallest vertebrate animal group in the world.

Reptile and Amphibian Families

There are three main groups of amphibians. These groups are frogs and toads, salamanders and newts, and caecilians. Each group has special features.

Frogs and toads are the largest amphibian group with more than 3,500 species. These animals have plump, rounded bodies. Frogs and toads have four legs. They use their hind, or back, legs for jumping. They do not have tails.

There are about 360 **salamander and newt** species. These animals look like lizards. They have long bodies and tails. They have four legs, too.

Caecilians look like large earthworms. They have long, legless bodies that are covered with rings. Caecilians have very sharp teeth. There are about 160 caecilian species.

There are four main groups of reptiles. These groups are lizards and snakes, turtles and tortoises, crocodiles and alligators, and tuataras.

The largest reptile group is **lizards and snakes**. There are about 3,000 lizard species and 2,700 snake species. These animals have large mouths. Many have forked tongues. They have long, scaly bodies. Lizards have short legs.

There are about 200 species of **turtles and tortoises**. Turtles have tough, bony shells that protect their bodies. They do not have teeth. They have hard beaks for tearing food.

Crocodiles and alligators are large animals with bony plates on their backs. They have short legs and long tails. Their long snouts are lined with sharp teeth. There are about twelve crocodile species and ten alligator species.

There are only two **tuatara** species. These animals look like lizards with spines, or spikes, on their backs and tails.

Reptile and Amphibian Appearances

Reptiles and amphibians come in many sizes and colors. Some are brightly colored. Others are dull. Many can change their body color to blend in with their environment.

Reptiles and amphibians share some special body features. Still, each species has **adapted** to its environment.

An amphibian begins its life as larva. Larvae look different from adults. They live in water. Larvae have **gills** to breathe. They have a tail to help them swim. They have small teeth, too. Adult amphibians' bodies are adapted to live on land and in the water.

Frog larvae are called tadpoles. When tadpoles become adults, they grow legs and their tail disappears.

Amphibians have permeable skin. This means they take in oxygen and water through **capillaries**. Most amphibians do not drink water. They soak water through their skin instead. Amphibian skin produces slime. This slime protects the animal from drying out.

Reptiles have dry, tough skin that is covered with scales. Most reptiles are green, brown, or gray. This color helps them blend into their surroundings. Some reptiles are brightly colored. They may be blue, yellow, orange, or red. These colors are a warning sign to predators. Reptiles shed their skin as they grow.

Reptiles have patterns on their skin to help them blend in with trees, shrubs, and grass.

Blue poison dart frogs grow between 1.2 to 1.8 inches (3 and 4.5 centimeters) long.

Fast Facts

The smallest amphibian is a type of poison dart frog that is only 0.5 inch (1.3 centimeters) long and weighs less than 1 ounce (28 grams). The largest amphibian is the Japanese giant salamander. It is 6 feet (1.8 meters) long and weighs 140 pounds (63 kilograms).

Reptiles and amphibians use the **Jacobson's organ** to detect smells.

Ancient Amphibian and Reptile Relics

Scientists use **fossils** to learn about animal history. The oldest amphibian fossils date back 350 million years. Scientists believe amphibians were the first vertebrate animals to live on land.

Many scientists believe amphibians developed from **lobe-finned** fish. These fish used their fins to walk on land for short periods of time. Over time, these fish adapted to life on land. Their fins became legs. The first modern amphibians lived about 230 million to 63 million years ago.

Albertosaurus was a large meat-eating reptile. An adult albertosaurus was about 25 to 30 feet (7.6 to 9.1 meters) long.

Reptile fossils date back 310 million to 275 million years. Scientists believe reptiles developed from amphibians. Reptiles adapted to life on land. They had tough skin and hard-shelled eggs. They could live in warm, dry places.

Reptiles were the most common animals on Earth during the **Mesozoic Era**. This time is also called the Age of the Reptiles. Tyrannosaurus and brachiosaurus are two of the reptiles that lived during this era.

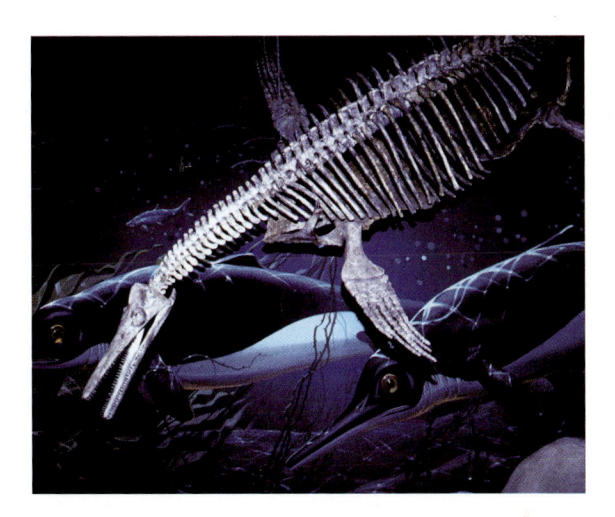

Ichthyosaurs were reptiles that lived in the ocean millions of years ago. They breathed air and gave birth to live young.

Amphibian fossils are found all over the world.

Fast Facts

Tuataras are sometimes called "living fossils." They are the only living species of *rhynchocephalid* reptiles. Tuataras have not changed much over the past 200 million years.

The *labyrinthodont* was one of the first amphibians. It appeared about 374 to 360 million years ago.

Life Cycle

Turtles lay between 1 and 200 eggs at one time. Larger turtles lay more eggs than smaller turtles.

Most amphibians hatch from eggs. Female frogs and toads lay eggs. The male frog or toad then **fertilizes** the eggs. Some amphibians fertilize the eggs still inside the female's body. Salamanders, newts, and caecilians belong to this group. Females lay many eggs at one time.

Most eggs are laid in water or moist areas. Fish-like larvae hatch from the eggs. Larvae do not look like adult amphibians. They have gills and a tail. Some larvae have small limbs. Young amphibians pass through **metamorphosis** before they become adults. They develop lungs and lose their gills during metamorphosis. Tadpoles are frog larvae.

Most reptiles hatch from eggs, too. Male reptiles fertilize eggs still inside the female's body. Turtles, crocodiles and alligators, tuataras, and some lizards and snakes lay their eggs on land. Others do not lay their eggs until the young are ready to hatch. A few snake and lizard species give birth to live young. Young reptiles look like small adult reptiles. Young reptiles grow slowly. They keep growing their entire lives.

Spotted salamanders can lay as many as 300 eggs at one time.

Lizard Lairs and Salamander Shelters

Reptiles and amphibians live in most parts of the world. They do not live in Antarctica. Some reptiles and amphibians live in forests. Others live in underground burrows. Many live in tropical regions.

Frogs and toads may live near water. Others, such as the red-eyed tree frog, live in trees. Some burrow underground.

The eastern spadefoot toad spends most of its time buried under soil.

Spadefoot toads have a spadelike feature on their hind foot. This "spade" helps the toad dig in loose soil for shelter. Some amphibians spend their entire lives in the water. Mudpuppies are large salamanders that use gills to breathe under water.

Mudpuppies can grow up to 18 inches (46 cm) long.

Most lizards live on the ground. They may also live in trees. These lizards have adapted special toes for grasping. Other lizards live in burrows. These lizards often have short legs. This helps them move more easily underground.

Some lizards, such as marine iguanas, live under water. They rest on rocks or sand. Other lizards, such as the Tibetan frog-eyed gecko, live in the desert. These animals do not like bright lights. They live under the sand during the day. They come out at night.

The crested iguana is found on the islands of Fiji in the southern Pacific Ocean.

Marine iguanas live on the Galapagos Islands. They are the only lizards that swim in the ocean.

Fast Facts

Snakes cannot live in places where the ground is frozen all year. They do not live in **polar** regions or mountains. There are no snakes in Ireland or New Zealand.

North America is home to more salamander and newt species than any other continent. No caecilians live in North America. They live only in tropical regions.

Snake Snacks and Frog Fare

Most reptiles and amphibians are carnivores. This means they are meat-eating animals. They eat fish or birds, for example. Reptiles and amphibians may be insectivores. This means they eat insects. Some amphibian larvae, lizards, and turtles mainly eat plants.

Crocodile and alligator species are carnivores. These reptiles drag their **prey** under water. Crocodiles and alligators tear pieces from the dead animal. They may swallow the prey whole, too. Snakes are carnivores. They eat their prey whole.

Garter snakes eat grasshoppers, earthworms, frogs, toads, and small birds and mammals.

Their jaws spread open so wide they can eat animals twice the size of their own heads. Some snakes use venom, or poison, to kill their prey. Other snakes are constrictors. This means they wrap their bodies around their prey and squeeze until the animal stops breathing. Other reptiles grab their prey and eat it live.

Some salamanders have no lungs. They breathe through their skin.

Adult amphibians are carnivores. Most frogs, toads, salamanders, and newts use their tongues to catch prey. These amphibians wait for prey to come nearby. Then, they flick their sticky tongues at the prey. They snap up the prey and pull it back to their mouths. Caecilians eat earthworms and insects that burrow underground. Caecilians slowly approach their prey. When they are very near their prey, caecilians capture it with a bite.

The alligator snapping turtle is the largest freshwater turtle in the world.

Fast Facts

The alligator snapping turtle has a bright red tongue. This tongue looks like a worm. The turtle opens its mouth and wriggles its tongue to catch prey. Fish think the tongue is a worm and swim into the turtle's mouth.

Aquatic, or water, salamanders hunt prey. They snap their mouths closed around prey. They suck in both the prey and water. The water leaves their mouth before it closes.

Ringed salamanders eat small invertebrates such as earthworms, insects, snails.

Threatened Reptiles and Amphibians

Animals that are in danger of becoming **extinct** are called endangered. This means that there are so few of the species that they need protection in order to survive. People are not allowed to hunt endangered animals in the United States.

There are many endangered reptiles and amphibians. In some cases, their habitat has become too **polluted** and unhealthy. Other habitats have disappeared. Some reptiles and amphibians have been overhunted. Humans who collect eggs also cause these animals harm.

Many scientists believe pollution and habitat loss is one reason why some species of reptiles and amphibians are becoming more rare.

18

The hawksbill turtle lives in warm waters between Africa, Asia, and North America. This turtle is hunted for its shell. The biggest threat to hawksbill turtles is that their eggs are collected by humans for food or stolen by other animals. More than half of the eggs laid by one of these turtles is stolen. Their population is declining as a result. Today, many places have nature reserves where these turtles can safely breed.

Hamilton's frog is one of the rarest frog species in the world. There are between 400 and 800 Hamilton's frogs on Earth. This species lives on 600 square miles (1,554 square kilometers) of land on Stephen's Island, New Zealand. This habitat has lost plant life. This causes climate extremes. Scientists have moved a small number of these frogs to another location on the island. This may help the species survive.

Hawksbill turtle meat is poisonous. Eating the meat can make people ill.

Fast Facts

Tuataras have no natural **predators**. New Zealand's first settlers brought rats, dogs, and cats to the island. These animals killed many tuataras.

Deformed amphibians have been found in 44 states. Poisons found in the air, water, or ground harm them.

Pollution has caused some frogs in the United States to have extra legs or missing body parts.

Activities

Toad Hall

Toads have rough, warty skin. They live in dark, damp places. Toads are welcome garden guests. They can eat up to three times their body weight each day. Toads can eat about 15,000 insects in one gardening season. The following activity shows how to make a toad house that can be placed in a garden.

Materials

- one medium-sized clay pot
- one medium-sized clay saucer that is about 1 inch (2.5 cm) deep
- outdoor paint
- paintbrush
- garden shovel
- sand

1. Paint the clay pot with the outdoor paint. Be creative.
2. Find a moist, shady area in the garden. Be sure there are plenty of bugs in the area.
3. Dig a hole in the ground. The hole should be deep enough to bury about one-third of the pot.
4. Lay the pot on its side inside the hole. Fill the bottom of the pot with a layer of soil. Add sand to the soil. Toads enjoy digging in sand on hot days.
5. Dig another hole near the pot. Place the clay saucer inside the hole. Be sure the saucer is level with the ground.
6. Fill the saucer with water. Toads absorb water through their skin. They will sit in the water saucer.
7. Watch for toads to come out at night.

Toads are shy animals that hide during the day.

Alligator Adornment

Alligators have long, flat snouts. They have sharp teeth, too. They eat fish, frogs, birds, snakes, turtles, and mammals. The following activity shows how to make a papier-mâché alligator.

Materials

- green, red, white, and black paint
- paintbrush
- newspaper
- cardboard
- white tissue paper
- scissors
- tape
- white glue

1. Cut one sheet of newspaper in half along the fold. Roll one-half of the newspaper into a tube. Roll the other half into a cone.

2. Fold the tube so that one end is about 4 inches (10.2 cm) longer than the other end. Roll up the longer end so it is even with the shorter end. Tape the roll in place. This is the alligator's snout.

4. Place the folded side of the snout inside the cone. Be sure the "v" of the cone is on top. Tape together the two pieces.

6. Make two paper-ball eyes. Each ball should be about 1 inch (2.5 cm). Tape the eyes to the top of the alligator's snout.

7. Make two newspaper tube legs. Tape the tubes to the bottom of the alligator. Make sure about 1 inch (2.5 cm) of leg shows on each side.

8. Mix equal amounts of glue and water. Brush the mixture onto the alligator. Then, place two layers of white tissue on the alligator.

9. Paint the alligator's body green, the inside of its mouth red, and its eyes white with a black circle in the center. Paint the nostrils black.

10. Cut ten triangle teeth from the cardboard. Paint the triangles white. Glue the teeth to the alligator's snout.

Quiz

What have you learned about reptiles and amphibians? See if you can answer the following questions correctly.

1. What is the difference between reptiles and amphibians?
2. Name the main groups of reptiles and amphibians.
3. How long have reptiles and amphibians lived on Earth?
4. How do crocodiles and alligators catch prey?
5. What stage do young amphibians pass through before becoming adults?

Frogs are useful to humans. They eat pests such as flies and mosquitoes.

Answers: 1. Reptiles have dry, scaly skin. Amphibians have moist, smooth skin. 2. The main groups of reptiles are lizards and snakes, crocodiles and alligators, turtles and tortoises, and tuataras. The main groups of amphibians are frogs and toads, newts and salamanders, and caecilians. 3. Reptiles have lived on Earth for 310 million to 275 million years. Amphibians have lived on Earth for about 350 million years. 4. Crocodiles and alligators drag their prey under water. 5. Young amphibians pass through metamorphosis before becoming adults.

Further Reading

Miller-Schroeder, Pat. *Reptiles and Amphibians: Scales, Slime, and Salamanders (Science@Work)*. Austin, TX: Raintree Steck-Vaughn, 2000.

Sneddon, Robert and Adrian Lascom (illustrator). *What is a Reptile?* New York, NY: Little, Brown and Company, 2002.

Woods, Samuel G. and Jeff Cline (illustrator). *The Amazing Book of Reptile and Amphibian Records: The Largest, the Fastest, the Most Poisonous, and Many More!*. Blackbirch Marketing, 2000.

Web Sites

For more information about amphibians and reptiles, visit www.ssarherps.org

Learn more about the reptiles and amphibians living in North America at www.herpscope.com

Each lizard species has a different diet. For example, green iguanas only eat plants.

Glossary

adapted adjusted to a specific situation

capillaries fine, thin blood vessels

deformed a change in the way something naturally looks

extinct no longer living

fertilizes makes another animal able to produce young

fossils the rocklike remains of ancient plants and animals

gills organs used to breathe water for oxygen

habitat place where an animal lives in nature

Jacobson's organ an organ in the mouth that detects scents in the air

lobe-finned paired fins that are similar to limbs such as legs

Mesozoic Era period between 230 million and 63 million years ago

metamorphosis a change in appearance

polar located near the North Pole or South Pole

polluted made unfit or harmful

predators animals that eat the flesh of other animals

prey animals that are hunted for food

Index

alligators 7, 13, 16, 17, 21, 22

caecilians 6, 13, 15, 17, 22
crocodiles 7, 13, 16, 22

endangered 18

food 7, 19
fossils 10, 11
frogs 4, 6, 8, 9, 13, 14, 16, 17, 19, 21, 22

habitat 5, 18, 19

life cycle 12, 13
lizards 6, 7, 13, 14, 15, 16, 22, 23

newts 6, 13, 15, 17, 22

salamanders 6, 9, 13, 14, 15, 17, 22
skin 4, 5, 9, 11, 17, 20, 22
snakes 5, 7, 13, 15, 16, 17, 21, 22

toads 6, 13, 14, 16, 17, 20, 22
tortoises 7, 22
tuatara 7, 11, 13, 19, 22
turtles 7, 12, 13, 16, 17, 19, 21, 22